# WEAPONIZING YOUR FAITH

## SUPERNATURALLY EQUIPPED TO RECEIVE YOUR BREAKTHROUGH

## HARRISON HOUSE BOOKS BY JOSEPH Z

*The Spirit of Elijah*

*The Spirit of Elijah Study Manual*

*Weaponize Your Faith*

*Demystifying the Prophetic: Understanding the Voice of God for the Coming Days*

*Breaking Hell's Economy: Your Guide to Last-Days Supernatural Provision*

*Jesus and the Kingmakers*

*Origin of the Cosmic Battle*

# WEAPONIZING YOUR FAITH

## SUPERNATURALLY EQUIPPED TO RECEIVE YOUR BREAKTHROUGH

JOSEPH Z

Published by Harrison House Publishers

Shippensburg, PA 17257

ISBN 13 TP: 978-1-6675-1136-8

ISBN 13 eBook: 978-1-6675-1137-5

For Worldwide Distribution, Printed in the U.S.A.

1 2 3 4 5 6 7 8 / 29 28 27 26 25

# CONTENTS


**1** You Were Born for This Time 1

**2** Burn the Ships and Don't Look Back 15

**3** Write the Vision 25

**4** Delay Is Not Denial 39

**5** The Secret Weapon 47

About Joseph Z 58

# 1 YOU WERE BORN FOR THIS TIME

It must be said, and you must hear it. In a world of darkness, in a culture gone rogue, creating a slope for evil to plunge deeper into its own mire—society will arrive at a place of chronic desperation. Surely, God has a plan! Surely, God has something prepared to spring on the world at the last moment! He must have a secret weapon: His very best, the last line of defense, the accumulation of generations who have paved the way to where we are in blood. The great God of heaven certainly must have His plan and response to launch against this onslaught of darkness!

He does! It's you!

## GOD BELIEVES IN YOU

You are marked and called by God to stand in the blood of Jesus and take territory unlike any other time in history. This is it! We are at the 12th hour;

we are at the one-yard line, and He has chosen you to be alive during the most significant time in our history. No matter the cost, no matter the assaults, regardless of the global crises coming in wave after wave. Remember this—on a bad day, you are the best there is!

God is so smart and chose you to be present during this time. If you don't believe it, believe in the God who placed you on the planet. He believes in you and calls you to be the answer for this generation because Christ is in you, the hope of glory!

## YOU'RE MADE IN HIS IMAGE AND LIKENESS

One of the greatest lies the devil told goes to the beginning when Satan spoke to Eve in the Garden. "For God knows that in the day you eat of it your eyes will be opened, and you will be like God" (Genesis 3:5 AMPC). The devil attempted to persuade God's original children into believing a half-truth regarding their relationship with the Father and their identity. The devil's intent was to convince Adam and Eve that God was holding back something from them. The actual truth was they were already like God! "God said, 'Let Us make mankind in Our image, according to Our likeness'" (Genesis 1:26). God's very first action toward mankind was to bless them. God's first words were, "Be fruitful and multiply" (Genesis 1:28).

The devil's lies are the same lies today. He instills a sense that you don't deserve anything from God and that God is withholding something from you. This kind of thinking is a lie from hell! God has always desired that His kids occupy and take over the family business. God created it; He wants His family to run it all.

## YOUR PRESENCE SHOULD DEMAND AN EXPLANATION

When walking in the midst of a dark and perverse generation, remember you're different. The world is dead; you're alive. This means your presence should demand an explanation. Whenever you show up, Jesus just walked in, because He resides in you. It's your time for confidence—shake off the old grave-clothes, be loosed of everything that so easily entangles you, and run with endurance the race that is set before you. Just like Jesus, the author and finisher of our faith, who, for the joy set before Him, endured the shame. You, my friend, were that joy set before Him!

## IT'S ONLY FOREVER

A dear friend whom I loved and ministered with would often say, "Hey, it's only forever!" He graduated to heaven a few years ago. As I go through life and do everything possible to impact the world for Jesus, his words come back to me: "It's only forever." Knowing that you have an eternal destination is a comfort but also gives a sense of determination. Eternity is where we will receive the rewards or results of missed assignments. This personally gives me the drive to live for significance. In eternity, you will not be floating on a cloud or in a nebulous state of consciousness, barely recognizing other saints who have gone before you. What we have to look forward to, even on the lowest level, is absolutely amazing. It is not an abstract experience; it's far more real than the "here and now." Eternity is a place of rewards and new assignments for the righteous.

## KINGS AND PRIESTS

*And has made us kings and priests to His God and Father, to Him be glory and dominion forever and ever. Amen.*

—Revelation 1:6

*And He has on His robe and on His thigh a name written: KING OF KINGS AND LORD OF LORDS.*

—Revelation 19:16

Jesus is the King of kings and the Lord of lords. Understanding the meaning behind this is a wonderful and sobering thought. We are called to rule and reign forever with Jesus. We are kings and lords. He is the King of the kings and Lord of the lords!

*And as they heard these things, he added and spake a parable, because he was nigh to Jerusalem, and because they thought that the kingdom of God should immediately appear.*
*12 He said therefore, A certain nobleman went into a far country to receive for himself a kingdom, and to return. 13 And he called his ten*

*servants, and delivered them ten pounds, and*
*said unto them, Occupy till I come. [14] But his*
*citizens hated him, and sent a message after*
*him, saying, We will not have this man to*
*reign over us. [15] And it came to pass, that when*
*he was returned, having received the king-*
*dom, then he commanded these servants to*
*be called unto him, to whom he had given the*
*money, that he might know how much every*
*man had gained by trading. [16] Then came the*
*first, saying, Lord, thy pound hath gained ten*
*pounds. [17] And he said unto him, Well, thou*
*good servant: because thou hast been faithful*
*in a very little, have thou authority over ten*
*cities. [18] And the second came, saying, Lord,*
*thy pound hath gained five pounds. [19] And he*
*said likewise to him, Be thou also over five cit-*
*ies. [20] And another came, saying, Lord, behold,*
*here is thy pound, which I have kept laid up*
*in a napkin: [21] for I feared thee, because thou*
*art an austere man: thou takest up that thou*
*layedst not down, and reapest that thou didst*
*not sow. [22] And he saith unto him, Out of thine*
*own mouth will I judge thee, thou wicked ser-*

*vant. Thou knewest that I was an austere man, taking up that I laid not down, and reaping that I did not sow:* [23] *wherefore then gavest not thou my money into the bank, that at my coming I might have required mine own with usury?* [24] *And he said unto them that stood by, Take from him the pound, and give it to him that hath ten pounds.* [25] *(And they said unto him, Lord, he hath ten pounds.)* [26] *For I say unto you, That unto every one which hath shall be given; and from him that hath not, even that he hath shall be taken away from him.* [27] *But those mine enemies, which would not that I should reign over them, bring hither, and slay them before me.*

—Luke 19:11-27 KJV

*He who is faithful in what is least is faithful also in much; and he who is unjust in what is least is unjust also in much.* [11] *Therefore if you have not been faithful in the unrighteous mammon, who will commit to your trust the true riches?* [12] *And if you have not been faithful in what is another man's, who will*

> *give you what is your own?* [13] *No servant can serve two masters; for either he will hate the one and love the other, or else he will be loyal to the one and despise the other. You cannot serve God and mammon.*
>
> —Luke 16:10-13

## REIGNING OVER TERRITORY IN ETERNITY

This parable in Luke 19, as well as Luke 16:11, has prophetic implications. Rewards for how stewardship is handled here on earth will play out in eternity. Notice that the types of rewards involve ruling over territory—cities, to be exact. Please understand that you were not created to live in heaven. Adam was created to rule the earth. In the end, there will be a new heaven and a new earth. The new earth is where we will reside and begin ruling. Much like the Garden of Eden, man was told to tend to it and take dominion over it. It is highly likely that had Adam not fallen, he and Eve would have continued expanding the Garden until the entire earth was under their dominion. It could be that they would have continued into the solar system until they even occupied other planets, causing them to flourish as well. It's only speculation, but ruling and reigning with Jesus for eternity could mean we will be responsible for expanding God's kingdom to the ends of the universe. This might be how we would exercise our kingship and lordship. Who knows what He has in store for His sons and daughters after we get past this present age. The Book of Revelation states that we will reign forever and ever.

> *And there shall be no more curse, but the throne of God and of the Lamb shall be in it, and His servants shall serve Him. [4] They shall see His face, and His name shall be on their foreheads. [5] There shall be no night there: They need no lamp nor light of the sun, for the Lord God gives them light. And they shall reign forever and ever.*
>
> —Revelation 22:3-5

What we do here and now will determine the level of reigning we will experience in eternity.

# GOING RED

*And they overcame him by the blood of the Lamb and by the word of their testimony, and they did not love their lives to the death.*

—Revelation 12:11

Now is the time to stand up and enforce the covenant promises on this earth. You are called to rise in this time, overcome by the blood of the Lamb and the word of your testimony, and not love your life even unto death. This is the formula for overcoming. In reference to the blood of Jesus, His covenant, and all it provides, we use the phrase "going red." For many years, our ministry and audience have become known as the "Red Church." It is not a denomination, not a doctrine, just a simple understanding that anyone, anywhere, who is washed in the blood of Jesus will rise, regardless of doctrinal differences that are not heaven or hell issues.

If Jesus is your Lord and you're covered by His blood, I consider you part of the Red Church. We are His blood-bought body. We know our covenant rights. "Going red" is a statement declaring Jesus is Lord, and we are covered in His blood. We're "going red" no matter what circumstances we face. This also carries the idea that we are to take the covenant of God to the ends of the earth by preaching the gospel. This is the highest responsibility a believer has. You need to "go red" and take the message of Jesus to everyone you meet.

He who wins souls is wise, according to Proverbs. Why? Because lost souls are the only thing God does not have. Going Red means we take the gospel of Jesus to them, winning them to Christ and making disciples. A person being saved is the only true thing we can give to God. A person saved and matured in the things of God is more valuable to the Lord than finding a gold mine. To Him, it would resemble receiving an inheritance of untold value. Psalm 116:15 gives us insight into the value God places on His mature saints.

> *Precious in the sight of the Lord is the death of His godly ones.*
>
> —Psalm 116:15 NASB

> *Precious (important and no light matter) in the sight of the Lord is the death of His saints (His loving ones).*
>
> —Psalm 116:15 AMPC

The word "precious" in this verse is the Hebrew word *yaqar,* which means *costly*. This verse could read: "Costly in the sight of the Lord is the death of His godly saints."

When God loses a mature believer to the grave, although He is thrilled to receive them in eternity, the cost is great on this earth. Why? Because of their experience and wisdom, the abilities they possessed from years of maturing their gifts and knowing Him at a high level are no longer working on the earth. Within the global population, very few know God through a disciplined life of surrender, prayer, and consecration. Few are tenured warriors, accurately tuned in to the Holy Spirit, having weaponized faith from years of practice. These rare ones are highly effective agents for the kingdom and are not easily replaced. The Lord of heaven only has so many believers of this caliber in each generation.

Remember, two things make God rich:

1. Lost souls getting saved. Converts who are transformed into mature believers through discipleship.
2. A tenured saint who lives a long life enforcing God's will on earth. These individuals are highly valuable to the Lord.

Darker days are coming than we ever imagined. Supernatural, mature believers must meet the kind of darkness our society is facing. If Jesus tarries, the body of Christ must step into its full potential as an unbeatable global superpower, highly capable of thwarting the powers of darkness. Together, we can effectively destroy the works of the devil; should the catching away of the saints happen sooner than later, the kingdom of darkness would breathe a sigh of relief!

A fire-baptized church, red with the blood of Jesus, releases a punishment against the darkness that it cannot tolerate. The current plans of evil cannot prevail, with the church of Jesus Christ standing in the way.

Together, we can destroy strongholds over many lives and change the world. It begins with you. You are the answer.

# 2 BURN THE SHIPS AND DON'T LOOK BACK

*I love those who love me, and those who seek me diligently will find me.* [18] *Riches and honor are with me, enduring riches and righteousness.* [19] *My fruit is better than gold, yes, than fine gold, and my revenue than choice silver.* [20] *I traverse the way of righteousness, in the midst of the paths of justice,* [21] *that I may cause those who love me to inherit wealth, that I may fill their treasuries.*

—Proverbs 8:17-21

There is a phrase associated with Spanish Conquistador Hernando Cortés from 1519: "Burn the ships." This phrase encompassed his single objective—capturing the treasures of the Aztecs. History's view of Cortés has differing points of view. However, the phrase "burn the ships" was made famous in his order to sink his own ships as an open display of resolve to finish what he started. A point in attaining requires a mindset of "no return." This same principle applies to weaponizing your faith. It is a mindset of faith and endurance to endure hardship like a good soldier (see 2 Timothy 2:3-4). By enduring hardship, you should be ready to persist against opposition until you receive what you are contending for.

## THE MINDSET OF A FINISHER

Many people enjoy the beginning of a journey; however, halfway through, they want to exit or turn back. My wife, Heather, and I were recently reminiscing about the many sincere individuals along our journey who have started with us to reach massive amounts of people worldwide through media to make a global impact with the gospel. Nearly two decades later, most of these excited beginners are long gone. However, we will continue in our calling. It takes more than a starter mentality. You must develop the mindset of a finisher.

I recall the day my associate pastor used a phrase during the time of a great decision; he said, "I think we burn the ships and don't look back!" He was making a statement about a tremendous move we were contemplating for our organization. We decided to relocate; the result would be churches planted, Bible schools raised, and overseas outreach would become far more effective. His words of faith and boldness provided the final push to step out fearlessly and do what we all sensed was right.

Each of us, including me, has experienced the "tough it out," "suck it up," and the "grin and bear it" mentality, combined with the "what doesn't kill you makes you stronger" speeches. Although these phrases aren't incorrect, they are incomplete by God's standards. What they do not consider is our loving Father who loves to equip His children for their sake and His divine purposes.

## RELIGION IS A "BREAKTHROUGH" KILLER

Religion may cause us to forget the absolute loving favor of our Father, but relationship does not. Someone once said, "Metaphors reign where mysteries reside." This simple saying is a great example of religion's way of thinking. It bases its point of view on the experiences of others rather than an encounter of your own. When you try to live off of someone else's experience, good or bad, you will never own it.

Therefore, metaphors come into use. Tragedy happens, and the response so often is, "Well, you just never know what God is going to do." Or someone becomes ill and succumbs to death, and religion gives well-meaning but hollow answers. "It must not have been God's will to heal them." Or the ever-sad comment, "God just needed another angel in heaven." None of these sayings are biblical. However, due to a lack of revelation on what God's Word says on specific topics, religion is forced to come up with well-intended answers. This applies to a variety of issues.

First, we must understand what a breakthrough is. One way of describing it is "to step into a *more than enough* blessing." Webster's Dictionary defines a breakthrough as *an act or instance of moving through or beyond an obstacle.* To receive a breakthrough, you must be obedient to the Lord and then be positioned in the appointed place or at the appointed time, according to God's will, to receive it.

What is required for a breakthrough or to maintain it is a revelation of what God has said in His Word; it must become rock solid inside you and be applied to your situation. The most potent force of any breakthrough is when you know or recall information contained in the Word of God for your situation, and it seemingly becomes illuminated or revealed at just the "right" time. This becomes a revelation or supernaturally "revealed truth" and knowledge for you! Peter encountered this when Jesus asked the disciples, "Who do you say I am?" Peter was able to respond (because of a revelation), "You are the Christ!"

## REVELATION IS REQUIRED FOR BREAKTHROUGH

Many of our spiritual forefathers once stood exactly where you are—on the edge of something they could not see. We know about the powerful ways God used them because we know the end of their story, but they couldn't see it coming when they were living it. Instead, they chose to stand in hopeful expectation. Another way of saying *hopeful expectation* is using the term "faith." When you apply your revelation or "revealed truth" with hopeful expectation/faith, the outcome is a breakthrough!

Let's look at three of our spiritual forefathers and their stories.

## KING DAVID

David was once a mere shepherd boy, the greatest king Israel would ever know. Even his father considered him insignificant. In 1 Samuel 16, God told Samuel the next king would be the son of Jesse. But when Jesse learned this, he showed Samuel all his sons—except David. It took Samuel specifically asking, "Are all the young men here?" before Jesse finally called David to meet Samuel. On that day, Samuel anointed David as the next king of Israel, and the Spirit of the Lord came upon David from that day forward (see 1 Samuel 16:13). One day, he was a shepherd. The next day, he was the future king.

Do you remember the story of David's cave days? In the days when all the promises were made, he killed Goliath and completed exploits, yet his father-in-law was hunting him. These were very difficult days for David. What we call his "cave days," David would have called those his "last days." However, he stood through it all and took his rightful place. His day came, he broke through, and he overcame the plans of darkness.

## ABRAHAM

The man often referred to as the father of our faith was once childless. It looked like Abraham and his wife, Sarah, would never have children. Their time had passed, and Sarah remained barren. Then, God blessed them with a child, Isaac. *Their faith brought forth a breakthrough!* However, God had one more major blessing, but first came obedience. Abraham was to take his blessed son and sacrifice him on an altar. Looking into the history of this story, you will discover that Isaac was between the ages of 23 and 30. He was a willing participant in this scenario. That is faith!

From Abraham's perspective, this could have been the end of his dream, but he faithfully obeyed anyway. God rewarded that obedience by sparing Isaac and promising to multiply Abraham's descendants. In Genesis 22:16-18, God promised Abraham that He would make his "descendants as the stars of the heaven and as the sand which is on the seashore."

Abraham was once childless, but God blessed "all nations on earth" through Abraham's offspring. His day came, he broke through, and he overcame the plans of darkness.

## JOSEPH

Joseph's journey to a breakthrough came after many hardships. First, he found himself in a pit (see Genesis 37), then a palace (see Genesis 39). That was short-lived before this innocent man of God was thrown into prison (see Genesis 39–40). Joseph went from disappointment to disappointment, from waiting to waiting, until his breakthrough came when he interpreted Pharaoh's dream (see Genesis 41). In one day, Joseph went from the dungeon to second in command over all the land of Egypt. There is a great insight into Joseph's journey as written for us in the Psalms.

> *He sent a man before them—Joseph—who was sold as a slave. [18] They hurt his feet with fetters, he was laid in irons. [19] Until the time that his word came to pass, the word of the Lord tested him.*
>
> —Psalm 105:17-19

The word of the Lord tested Joseph. How? Because Joseph knew he had a vision. God showed him his future, but everything he experienced leading up to the "Word" coming to pass was contrary. It must have been hard for Joseph not to throw in the towel. Thankfully, he didn't, and his day came. He broke through, and he overcame the plans of darkness.

Each of these spiritual forefathers' day came after God took them through a *season of preparation*. God had a calling on their life, but they needed to be ready to rise to the occasion when that breakthrough came.

Maybe you are in a *season of preparation*, too. Would you recognize it if you were? Are you struggling with feeling insignificant like David? Waiting on a heart's desire like Abraham? Overwhelmed with trials and setbacks like Joseph? Maybe it's time to look at it differently; maybe it's your season of preparation.

God has a day of breakthrough for you, and age has nothing to do with it. Just like David, Abraham, and Joseph, your calling is at the door of your heart, crying out to come forth.

You may not see it yet, and you may question your circumstances and struggles, but never doubt that God has a call and a plan for your life. He is working through all these seemingly unplanned events and dreary days to position you for His moment of blessing.

Your season of preparation will bring with it opportunity if you do not give up. Choose today to stay the course. Like our spiritual forefathers, your day of breakthrough will change everything. Your day will come, and you will overcome the plans of darkness. This could be coming sooner than you think!

# 3 WRITE THE VISION

*Then the Lord answered me and said: "Write the vision and make it plain on tablets, that he may run who reads it. [3] For the vision is yet for an appointed time; but at the end it will speak, and it will not lie. Though it tarries, wait for it; because it will surely come, it will not tarry. [4] Behold the proud, his soul is not upright in him; but the just shall live by his faith."*

—Habakkuk 2:2-4

## WRITE YOUR VISION AND MAKE IT CLEAR

Your day of breakthrough has a purpose: to help you accomplish your life assignment. That's what you have from God. A job to do. He's assigned work that must be completed, and you'll need help to get it done. For any assignment, task, or responsibility, you need specific tools. Your day of breakthrough is that tool. But how do you know what that job is? How do you find it? When you find it, what do you do when your breakthrough hasn't yet come?

Habakkuk had questions, too. He sought an answer from God. In Habakkuk 2:2, God answered, "Write the vision and make it plain on tablets, that he may run who reads it."

God is giving us direction, a formula for approaching our tasks when unsure what to do next. In verse 3, He continues, "Though it tarries, wait for it; because it will surely come, it will not tarry."

## WRITE THE VISION DOWN

God has placed a dream in your heart, and you owe it to Jesus to pursue it. You also owe it to yourself to write it down. Habakkuk 2:2 shows us that power is attached to writing your vision down. It is a spiritual statement and a heightened clarity of that vision. Writing it down is a powerful and necessary tool. Writing your vision down also allows you to see your deepest desires written out before you visually.

God wants you to have your desires. The key is first to prioritize His desires. "But seek first the kingdom of God and His righteousness, and all these things shall be added to you" (Matthew 6:33). This is the proper order for receiving your desires the kingdom way.

To receive your desires, you must first understand that God made you. He knows what makes you tick—or, as one dear friend said, "God knows how to give you a buzz!" The kingdom approach seeks His ways of doing things first and righteousness. His ways are laid out for us in Scripture. If you desire His breakthrough to begin working dramatically in your life, you must follow the kingdom's "rules of engagement."

## RULES OF ENGAGEMENT

Simply put, you must be into the business of sowing and reaping. This creates a rhythm in God's economy that brings continuous victories. It is, however, the hidden vein of gold that you encounter when you seek first His kingdom through His way of doing things. Second, His righteousness is what you must also seek. This means knowing Jesus paid it all for you, and as you grow in the revelation of what He did and how righteous you are in Him, all these other things are added unto you! These things are the vein of gold—the things only God knows you truly desire. There are things you desire that you don't even know about! But God does—He wants to give you everything you never knew you wanted.

Once you have written down your known desires and vision, there is a process to pursue what you have written. Psalm 37:3-5 reveals a process of receiving the desires of your heart.

> *Trust in the Lord, and do good; so shalt thou dwell in the land, and verily thou shalt be fed.* [4] *Delight thyself also in the Lord: and he shall give thee the desires of thine heart.* [5] *Commit thy way unto the Lord; trust also in him; and he shall bring it to pass.*
>
> —Psalm 37:3-5 KJV

Verse 3, broken down, reads: trust in the Lord, do good, dwell in the land, and feed on *His faithfulness!*

## IT IS BETTER TO DO GOOD…THAN TO NOT

The first thing you must do is to trust in the Lord! God has this thing about being believed! He wants you to develop your trust in Him completely. Second, do good. That's an interesting thought. To simply do good. It makes me think of Steve Martin's quote from the movie *Dirty Rotten Scoundrels*:

> *"My gram-gram is the one who taught me it is better to be truthful and good…than to not."*
>
> —Steve Martin, *Dirty Rotten Scoundrels*

That quote makes me laugh every time because it is hilariously obvious. In fact, it is the truth—one way we approach the desires of our hearts is by doing good!

## YOUR PRESENCE SHOULD DEMAND AN EXPLANATION

Psalm 37:3 goes on to say, "dwell in the land." Another way of saying this would be, "Take dominion where you are!" Wherever you are, be there! I like saying it this way, "Your presence should demand an explanation!"

Taking your dominion is a way of enforcing the kingdom of God on this earth. Let's continue reading verse 3: "Feed on His faithfulness." Knowing God will always come through for you and show up every time is equivalent to not feeding worries and doubt. Instead, you are feeding on His consistency. Know this and meditate on it.

"Delight yourself also in the Lord, and He shall give you the desires of your heart" (Psalm 37:4). In this verse, we begin to see the words "delight yourself in the Lord." Webster's Dictionary defines "delight" as *a more permanent pleasure than joy.* Make God the most permanent pleasure in your life. Place more pleasure in God than in the things that make you happy. If you do this, the things that give you joy or the desires of your heart are given to you. "Commit your way to the Lord, trust also in Him, and He shall bring it to pass" (Psalm 37:5).

But wait, there's more! Part of delighting in the Lord and receiving the desires of your heart is giving them staying power and longevity. This comes from committing your way. All the above, including a focused commitment to the Lord, will cause Him to bring the fullness of your desires and purpose to pass. If you lean in, so will God. It's pretty awesome if you think about it.

## EXAMINE YOUR HEART

This process gives you focus for the journey ahead. Start by examining your heart. When God begins speaking to you, you might not immediately understand what He's saying. Take the time to hear all that God is doing inside you.

Don't feel overwhelmed. If you don't know what your life's about or where you're going, start with your desires. Write down your thoughts. For example, "God, I would like to see my life doing this," and "I would like to do that." Ask Him for understanding of what your life is about.

## ANYTHING WITH MORE THAN ONE HEAD IS A FREAK!

This is crucial because you need a one-mind, one-heart, one-head vision to lead you in one direction. You can't be double-minded about your vision. If you want to defeat a man's vision, give him two. When you have more than one vision, you will not only see the potential of division, but it will cause diversion. You need clarity, focus, and oneness. Anything with more than one head is considered a freak. Be single-minded!

If you are washed in the Word of God, you will see your desires line up with His commands. His words will provide clarity and direction so your heart's desires become clear and in agreement with His plans for your life.

Years ago, as I dove more into the scriptures, the Lord challenged me to write down the answers to these questions: What do I want out of life? Where do I want to go? My vision found clarity as I sought His direction for my life according to the Word of God. Yours will, too. Your desires will become more focused and develop as you stay in His Word. Then, when opportunity meets preparation, you'll recognize that God has developed your heart and placed you in your lane.

## ELEVATOR SPEECH

Remember to keep it simple. When we write down our vision, we need to keep it simple. God directed

Habakkuk to "make it plain" so it would be understandable.

In earlier times, messages were written down and passed between villages. Simplicity was key. A simple message could easily be understood with one look to a rider passing by quickly and simply re-told.

That's how you need to view your vision. It must be simple. Easily understood and quickly comprehended. Your plans are too complicated if you can't write a simple vision. You should be able to put your vision on a placard and hold it up; anyone passing by can understand what you're all about. My placard would read, "Building lives by the Word of God." That's my vision. Simple, uncomplicated, and easy to understand.

The placard then creates the foundation for your elevator pitch. In other words, what would be your answer if you had 60 seconds in an elevator to explain your vision? You should be able to explain what you do, who you are, and what you're about in simple bullet points or a quick explanation. My elevator speech is, "To build lives by the Word of God. I accomplish this through discipleship and media so the Word of God can run swiftly and be glorified."

Ultimately, you need one thing that identifies your life.

## JACK OF ALL TRADES, MASTER OF ONE

Have you ever heard the expression "Jack of all trades but master of none"? A better rendition of the expression would be "Jack of all trades but *master of one*." This means you should know little about everything but everything you can about one thing. Excel at something! When you give focus and training to the area you want to develop, your "elevator speech" about who, what, where, and why becomes simplified.

## YOU MUST STAND

In Habakkuk 2:3 (NIV), God followed His first two instructions by assuring Habakkuk that the vision is for an appointed time: "For the revelation awaits an appointed time; it speaks of the end and will not prove false. Though it linger, wait for it; it will certainly come and will not delay."

Let's say you've written your vision down. You kept it simple. You've waited, but nothing seems to be happening. This desire is so strong, burning a hole in your heart, but it still hasn't come to pass. So what's going on?

God is telling Habakkuk here that His plans have an "appointed time." That time hasn't come yet. But it will. Notice God's command: "Though it linger, wait for it; it will certainly come."

The fulfillment of your vision is coming, even though it hasn't arrived yet. God's direction for us at this moment is to wait. You've prayed, written it down, and now you stand.

## SEE YOURSELF VICTORIOUS WITH THE PRIZE

Ephesians 6:10-17 gives clarity on what it means to stand.

> *Finally, my brethren, be strong in the Lord, and in the power of his might. [11] Put on the whole armour of God, that ye may be able to stand against the wiles of the devil. [12] For we wrestle not against flesh and blood, but against principalities, against powers, against the rulers of the darkness of this world,*

*against spiritual wickedness in high places.* [13]
*Wherefore take unto you the whole armour*
*of God, that ye may be able to withstand in*
*the evil day, and having done all, to stand.* [14]
*Stand therefore, having your loins girt about*
*with truth, and having on the breastplate of*
*righteousness;* [15] *and your feet shod with the*
*preparation of the gospel of peace;* [16] *above*
*all, taking the shield of faith, wherewith ye*
*shall be able to quench all the fiery darts of*
*the wicked.* [17] *And take the helmet of salva-*
*tion, and the sword of the Spirit, which is the*
*word of God.*

—Ephesians 6:10-17 KJV

The word "stand" is mentioned three times in this passage and has the contextual meaning of *seeing yourself victorious and receiving the prize.* This passage is all about the whole armor of God, preparing and going to battle. Stand means to stand as if receiving the trophy or reward for beating the opposition in the gladiator arena.

*Stand*—it doesn't mean endure and take the punishment; you might get through it at some undetermined time in the future. No! That is not what stand means. It means to see yourself victorious going into the fight. When going into the process of attaining those desires of your heart, you stand seeing yourself victorious until you step into that reality.

Something supernatural happens when a man or woman writes down their vision and stands on it. You wait with expectancy, confidence, and knowledge, knowing the appointed hour may not be here at this moment; however, in faith, you have it, and in the natural, it's coming.

Do not faint. Stand on the Word of God, mix it with your faith, and see yourself receiving the prize. There's an appointed time for you. Even though it lingers, wait! It will certainly come!

# 4 DELAY IS NOT DENIAL

*For the vision is yet for an appointed time; but at the end it will speak, and it will not lie. Though it tarries, wait for it; because it will surely come, it will not tarry.*

—Habakkuk 2:3

## TARRYING CAN BE PART OF THE VISION

Tarrying is something that can be part of the journey. However, you are not always called to stay there! This can manifest in the form of a trial or just becoming weary in well-doing. This is where you lean in. Trials don't always last; they are not able to last forever. Do you know what is designed to last forever? You! God designed you never to experience that kind of difficulty and delay. The "fall of man" allowed this type of disappointment to reign on earth. Through the blood and victory of Jesus, we are called to stand up in defiance of this fallen world. Don't be fooled; don't give in to the mirage of this world. If you do not faint, you will see victory.

## THE BATTLE ISN'T OVER UNTIL YOU WIN!

A quote I often use while speaking: "The battle isn't over until you win!" Arm yourself with the mindset that the battle isn't over because you haven't seen the victory yet. With this mindset, you will begin to take more ground in your heart and the natural. God never designed you to fail or fall into despair. Be armed with the Word of God and put some intensity into your believing. The enemy of your soul and the spirit of this age has no response for a believer who mixes their faith with the Word of God and speaks it out!

Sometimes, people misidentify what they are going through. These could call *denial* a river in Egypt! (Pun intended.)

During those "in-between" times, you must keep yourself encouraged. If the enemy can get you discouraged or into a place of disbelief, you will begin to lose the momentum on what you are believing for. It is a form of "abortion" to the seed that has been placed in you by the Holy Spirit to be birthed in this world. It reminds me of an article I once read regarding the common survival traits of those lost in the wilderness. Among several traits that stood out to me most was that many people who make it after being lost in the wilderness end up with a good sense of humor.

## HAVE A SENSE OF HUMOR

Someone may ask, "A good sense of humor! Are you kidding me?" Well, think about it. It makes sense to me on several levels. In my estimation, the best trait is to start laughing in faith while suffering through the worst conditions! You should give joy a voice! Imagine the kingdom of darkness throwing everything they have at you, and your response is to laugh. It would confuse them! It would make them question their tactics. So—*ha ha ha!*

## THE ART OF FAITH AND PATIENCE

> *And we desire that each one of you show the same diligence to the full assurance of hope*

> *until the end, [12] that you do not become sluggish, but imitate those who through faith and patience inherit the promises.*
>
> —Hebrews 6:11-12

I firmly believe you can limit the time you have to wait. You have far more authority than you may realize. Let's discuss the power of patience.

Patience, in so many words, means to remain consistently the same no matter what is happening in the world around you. Circumstances may change, but regarding the promise of God, you will not be changed. Faith is the substance of things hoped for, the evidence of things not seen. Once you have substance and evidence of what you cannot yet grasp with your hands, this is where stubborn patience is employed. I promise you, the man or woman of God who refuses to step away from the promise and stays consistently the same while using the standard principle of seeing yourself receiving the prize will never lose. It's not possible.

Let's add some hot sauce to what we discussed. Combine all this with the intensity of prayer, which will force obstacles out of the way.

The path of the righteous is supposed to be brighter and brighter until the full light of day, meaning you are meant to go from glory to glory in your journey. The issue is that most people never develop the practices or incorporate the combination of principles listed to create "staying power" in their lives. Staying power is applying consistent pressure and not letting up to attain what you first began to believe for. You must stay encouraged even when you don't see your circumstances changing. You may be on a road headed toward your destination, but you can't see the destination yet. Even though the landscape looks the same as when you left and doesn't seem to change, you know if you keep going, you are getting closer, and soon the destination will appear in the distance until you arrive!

A praying believer is dangerous to the plans of the devil. It makes the weak strong and the foolish wise. It gives impossible breakthroughs to the average person if they give themselves over to the intensity of prayer. I like to say, "On a bad day, you're called to be the best there is!" The praying believer is the best there is.

## BINDING YOURSELF TO THE LORD

What we're called to do during this time of tarrying is to stand and *wait well*. Psalm 27:14 says, "Wait on the Lord; be of good courage, and He shall strengthen your heart; wait, I say, on the Lord!" We see the importance of waiting on God throughout Scripture. Isaiah 40:31 says, "But those who wait on the Lord shall renew their strength; they shall mount up with wings like eagles, they shall run and not be weary, they shall walk and not faint." This is an active, purposeful waiting. It binds us with God's will.

In Hebrew, "waiting on the Lord" means *to bind together with the twisting as with wire.* When you wait on the Lord, you take your life, desires, and heart, then bind yourself with the Lord. When you're at the point in the process where you don't see your vision manifesting, you must twist your life tightly to God. You bind yourself to Him. "A cord of three strands is not quickly broken" (Ecclesiastes 4:12 AMP).

As you bind yourself to the Lord, you move closer to Him. In this process, you become one with the Lord in your thinking. Your heart, mind, emotions, and calling intertwine with God's will. This isn't a time of sitting around until God moves. It's a time of moving closer to Him.

In the middle of Habakkuk 2:3, it says, "Though it tarries, wait for it; because it will surely come." God cannot lie. His words are always true. If He says it's coming, it's coming. It doesn't matter what happens in the meantime; whether we're amid the apocalypse or hell freezes over, the Word of God never lies. The vision is coming. It does not depend on your family situation, financial situation, successes or failures, mistakes or regrets. God's promise remains unaffected if you do not quit and continue to bind yourself with the Lord. Do not be discouraged. Trust God's process and stay faithful. Your appointed time and breakthrough are coming.

## DO NOT LISTEN TO ANYTHING THAT LIMITS YOU

Creation will continue roaring, shaking, and quaking because it is waiting for God's manifest sons and daughters to complete the Great Commission. We must send people, go, and experience our breakthrough to spread the gospel in Jesus' name. We must stop listening to teachings that limit and hinder this.

We move toward fulfilling the Great Commission by following the guidelines in Joshua 1:8. We keep the Word of God in our mouths, then our minds, and finally, our actions. Seek the Lord as you write your vision and make it plain. Then, stand on that vision, wait in faith, and bind yourself to the Lord. Your vision will come to fruition.

# 5 THE SECRET WEAPON

> *But solid food belongs to those who are of full age, that is, those who by reason of use have their senses exercised to discern both good and evil.*
>
> —Hebrews 5:14

Hebrews 5:14 talks about maturity. One sign of spiritual maturity is exercising your senses, referencing your natural physical impulses, emotions, and persuasions. Your five senses are significant players in this. Notice it says their senses are exercised through "reason of use," which means a disciplined practice of putting what you see, smell, taste, touch, and hear under the truth of the Word of God.

The point is that the natural ability to navigate life through maturity must regularly be subject to a renewed soul with a revelation from the spirit. We are to read our Bibles and pray daily in a disciplined way.

## CHARACTER

Character is both emotional and behavioral development. Along with maturity, it is vital to see a breakthrough. It is the staying force keeping a person on the rails. Without character, every gifted person will eventually falter horribly. Character is the opposite of being led off by wild experiences. It is empowered by the Word of God—your solid foundation.

## CARNAL AND NATURAL-MINDED PEOPLE WALK IN BLINDNESS!

> *I say then: Walk in the Spirit, and you shall not fulfill the lust of the flesh.*
>
> —Galatians 5:16

Walking in the Spirit means walking in God's Word. Jesus, after all, said His words were Spirit in John 6:63. What must be understood is the flesh. What does the Bible mean by flesh or carnality? The flesh is a way of thinking that opposes God's Word. The flesh is a mindset not led by the Word of God but by the five senses.

A good example of this would be a person who looks at the natural by only watching the news and what are common, normal markers to navigate through life. Sadly, from their intellect and natural persuasions, most people live 100 percent of their time on earth. They believe nothing unless it is scientifically verified and proven from every angle. Even then, they look through the meat glasses of carnality.

## THE RICH MAN AND LAZARUS

> *There was a certain rich man who was clothed in purple and fine linen and fared sumptuously every day. [20] But there was a certain beggar named Lazarus, full of sores, who was laid at his gate, [21] desiring to be fed with the crumbs which fell from the rich man's table. Moreover the dogs came and licked his sores. [22] So it was that the beggar died, and was carried by the angels to Abraham's bosom. The rich man also died and was buried. [23] And being in torments in Hades, he lifted up his eyes and saw Abraham afar off, and Lazarus in his bosom. [24] Then he cried and said, "Father Abraham, have mercy on me, and send Lazarus that he may dip the tip of his finger in water and*

> *cool my tongue; for I am tormented in this flame.” 25 But Abraham said, “Son, remember that in your lifetime you received your good things, and likewise Lazarus evil things; but now he is comforted and you are tormented. 26 And besides all this, between us and you there is a great gulf fixed, so that those who want to pass from here to you cannot, nor can those from there pass to us.” 27 Then he said, “I beg you therefore, father, that you would send him to my father’s house, 28 for I have five brothers, that he may testify to them, lest they also come to this place of torment.’ 29 Abraham said to him, “They have Moses and the prophets; let them hear them.” 30 And he said, “No, father Abraham; but if one goes to them from the dead, they will repent.” 31 But he said to him, “If they do not hear Moses and the prophets, neither will they be persuaded though one rise from the dead.”*
>
> —Luke 16:19-31

Consider the rich man and Lazarus. Interestingly, part of this story parallels what Jesus conveyed about those who see the world only through the natural lens.

Amazingly, Jesus, by telling the story of Lazarus and the rich man, comes to the part where the rich man, who was in hell, begs Father Abraham to send an angel or someone back from the dead to tell the rich man's living relatives about the horrors of hell. This story shows what happens to departed souls who have not called on the Name of the Lord. It also conveys a powerful truth even through the dazzling of the five senses, with shocking empirical evidence of the supernatural, such as someone coming back from the dead to testify of what awaits after death. Even such an encounter would not make the recipients believe if they did not already believe the scriptures. Again, as Abraham stated in Luke 16:31, "If they do not hear Moses and the prophets, neither will they be persuaded though one rise from the dead."

Miracles without the Word of God following do not provide sustaining power. The rich man asked for the equivalent of his idea of the ultimate magic act—shock them, dazzle them, and then they will believe. Ultimately, this was his thought process and belief system.

## ABRAHAM'S RESPONSE

> *And he said, "No, father Abraham; but if one goes to them from the dead, they will repent."*[31] *But he said to him, "If they do not hear Moses and the prophets, neither will they be persuaded though one rise from the dead."*
>
> —Luke 16:30-31

The rich man pleaded and negotiated with Abraham, saying *if you will send Lazarus or send someone back from the dead—then people would believe!* The rich man wrongly said *God has not done a good enough job!* The rich man might as well have said, "If you would do it the way I am saying to do it, then they would listen!"

The rich man displayed his hardness of heart, saying that if you give them irrefutable scientific evidence, they will believe. Where the words of Jesus clearly state, "Blessed are those who believe without seeing" (see John 20:29).

God desires to be believed without Him painting things in crayon for the five senses to grasp in every imaginable way. However, if you read and believe the Bible, all things available to know by the Spirit will become illuminated.

## MAN LOOKS TO THE NATURAL, BUT GOD OPERATES BY FAITH

My point in comparing the two scenarios is that man always looks to the natural or carnal side for evidence and truth. In contrast, God is a Spirit, and those who worship Him must do so in spirit and truth! (See John 4:24.) Another way of looking at this would be to say that God is more interested in you believing Him before He has to prove Himself to you.

Remember Thomas, who said, "Unless I see in His hands the print of the nails, and put my finger into the print of the nails, and put my hand into His side, I will not believe" (John 20:25).

In a gracious accommodation, Jesus allowed Thomas to do those very things (see John 20:27). I believe Jesus allowed this because He already had a relationship with Thomas. What is vital, however, is not to be led by the carnal point of view but rather by a point of view filled with and operated by the Spirit of God.

## MIND RENEWAL

> *And do not be conformed to this world, but be transformed by the renewing of your mind, so that you may prove what the will of God is, that which is good and acceptable and perfect.*
>
> —Romans 12:2 NASB

In the life of a believer, there is a process of mind renewal called discipleship. Through growth in discipleship comes a level of spiritual activation by the infilling of the Holy Spirit.

## THE FIVE SENSES

Your soul needs polishing! How is this accomplished? Let's look at Hebrews 5:14 once again for the answer: "But solid food belongs to those who are of full age, that is, those who by reason of use have their senses exercised to discern both good and evil."

The word "senses" here means *to perceive with the external senses or five senses*: what you can touch, smell, hear, taste, or see. Human beings have developed these senses for their entire lives. Suddenly, we come into a relationship with the living God, which challenges our five senses. God is not logical! He is the faith God. This natural world wants us to remain dependent on our five senses.

## MIRROR OR MIRAGE

The antidote to a dim soul is polishing the glass! Without this polishing, a mirage will form. The mirage is powerful—like gravity for the carnal. Suppose a believer runs for the mirage rather than the mirror. In that case, believers will display no recognizable difference between themselves and the world.

The saddening end of chasing the mirage will ultimately make your heart cold. Therefore, many believers are depressed or struggle with their faith. When difficulties inevitably arise, what they have planted in their hearts immediately stands up in defiance to faith and the life of God.

Fear, sorrow, anger, hopelessness, and unbelief will manifest in the place of faith. In this stage, when a crisis hits, the carnal will sometimes frantically pray or bring God into focus. Usually mixing their prayers with accusations toward God or from a misinformed and wounded heart, asking, "Why?" Or, "What have You done or allowed, God?" When truthfully, their lens has been habitually darkened to respond from the flesh and not in faith.

## THE MIRROR EXPOSES THE MIRAGE

The mirror is vastly different from the mirage. The mirror is the reflection of who the believer is in Christ! It is the Word of God mixed with faith! I have often stated the gospel you hear preached is correct! But it is only complete once it is working through you!

## EFFECTS OF THE COMPLETE GOSPEL

The mirror shows who a person is and how to act. It sensitizes you to the love and leading of the Holy Spirit. It offers you life and overcoming power that dumbfounds the carnal. It fosters peace that surpasses natural logic! Things can go super bad, but because of focusing on the mirror, victory is experienced even in difficulty.

The mirror is for believers. When someone turns to Jesus as their means of salvation, they receive an unveiled face, and they can then behold the glory of the Lord as reflected and radiant in the gospel.

## REAL TRANSFORMATION

The more you behold, the more you are changed into what you're beholding! The mirror takes the weak and says, "You are so strong! In Christ, you are perfectly righteous! In Christ, you're as holy as you're going to get!" On a bad day, the mirror says, "In Christ, you are the best there is!" The mirror declares you a winner! When you soak and meditate on the reflection it presents, you will see the change that has already been done inside you and manifests to the outside!

The real answer is to be preemptive by mixing the Word of God with your faith today, right now! Become prepared for what's around the corner by transforming into the image you see in the mirror. It's effortless. All that's required is to behold! Habitually cut out the distractions! Spend time with the mirror, and your life will change from the inside to the outside!

# ABOUT JOSEPH Z

Joseph Z is an author, broadcaster, Bible teacher, and international prophetic voice. Before the age of nine, he began encountering the voice of God through dreams and visions. Joseph has dedicated his life to preaching the gospel around the world. He and his wife, Heather, are founders of Z Ministries, a media and conference-based ministry in Colorado, USA.